Gilman Joslin

Joslin's terrestrial and celestial globes

Gilman Joslin

Joslin's terrestrial and celestial globes

ISBN/EAN: 9783337733469

Printed in Europe, USA, Canada, Australia, Japan

Cover: Foto ©ninafisch / pixelio.de

More available books at **www.hansebooks.com**

JOSLIN'S

TERRESTRIAL AND CELESTIAL

GLOBES.

—∘∘⁊⊶⊷∘∘⊷—

GILMAN JOSLIN & SON,

MANUFACTURERS AND DEALERS, 5 MT. VERNON AVE.,

BOSTON, MASS.

USEFULNESS OF GLOBES.

THE importance of globes, both as articles of school and household furniture, has long been greatly under-estimated.

Until within a few years they were to be found, with rare exceptions, only among our colleges and leading academies, with occasionally one in some public or private library, and were regarded almost in the light of a curiosity by the large mass of people.

In these days of popular education, however, the importance and necessity of their use in framing correct ideas in the minds of children at the outset, together with their value for subsequent reference and study, has become much more widely recognized, and has led to their general introduction into schools of all grades.

It is an important fact in favor of such general introduction that almost all children and many grown people manifest *intense interest and surprise* when they see a globe for the *first time.* They then seem to drink in at once an entirely new idea of the correct shapes and true *relative positions* of the various countries, their false notions of which have been produced by the exclusive study of maps printed on flat surfaces, and which are, on that account, necessarily somewhat incorrect.

As a matter of fact, the presence of a globe in the schoolroom, even though not a single lesson be given upon it, has been found to be of the greatest assistance; for, having it constantly before them, the scholars acquire many and correct ideas which could not be gathered from books, the impressions from which are of valuable and lasting service to them.

As an example of the increased consideration now being given to this subject, we may say that the City of Boston, whose schools are universally conceded to be among the foremost in this country, has recently purchased for their use *one or more of Joslin's Globes for every school-room above the primary grade throughout the city.* Moreover, the Joslin Globe was selected after a critical examination by the Committee of all globes in the market.

For library or office use a globe is no less valuable, showing, as it does at a glance, the true relative situations of Political and Geographical Divisions, Cities, etc., the world over.

Some of the advantages of these globes are : They may be depended upon as *accurate,* the plates having lately been revised to correspond with all recent political changes. All the maps are printed *directly from copper plates*, and are not lithographed. The meridians are *accurately graduated. The varnish is warranted not to crack or peel off,* a common failing. The stands are thoroughly and firmly fitted together, and the *general workmanship throughout* is of the *first order.*

Finally, it will be our constant endeavor to maintain the reputation which our globes have long enjoyed for superior accuracy, durability, and beauty, and to merit on that account a liberal share of public patronage.

With these few introductory remarks upon the general usefulness and importance of the globe, we will proceed to describe how to use a globe in the working of problems, etc.

GILMAN JOSLIN & SON.

HOW TO USE A GLOBE.

1. A **Terrestrial Globe** is a ball or sphere, representing the earth. Upon its surface are drawn the natural divisions of land and water, — continents, islands, capes, mountains, oceans, lakes, bays, rivers, etc.; it also represents the political divisions of countries, and the lines of latitude and longitude.

2. The **Axis** of the earth is represented by the iron rod which passes through the centre of the globe, and upon which it turns.

3. The **Poles** of the earth are the two ends of the axis; one is called the North or Arctic Pole, and the other the South or Antarctic Pole.

4. The **Equator** is a circle passing around the globe at equal distances from the poles. It divides the globe into the Northern and Southern hemispheres.

5. The **Equinoctial** is the equator extended to the heavens. When the sun is crossing the equinoctial, the days and nights are equal all over the world.

6. All **Circles** on the globe are supposed to be divided into 360 equal parts, called *degrees*.

7. The **Brass Meridian** is the circle of brass within which the globe turns on its axis. One half of this meridian is graduated from the equator to the poles; that is, the point over the equator is 0, and the point over the poles is 90; this enables us to find the latitude of a place. The other half is from 0 at the poles to 90 at the equator; this is so that we can elevate the pole to the latitude of the place.

8. **Meridians** of longitude are semicircles extending from pole to pole, and cut the equator at right angles. Beginning at Greenwich, which is called the first meridian, there is on the globe a meridian every 15 degrees; these correspond to the hours of time, dividing the globe into 24 equal parts.

9. The **Longitude** of a place is the distance of the meridian passing through it from the first meridian, reckoned in degrees on the equator. Longitude is either east or west, according as the place is east or west of the first meridian. The figures on the north side of the equator express the degrees of longitude, and are reckoned from Greenwich east and west from 0° to 180°. The Roman letters on the south side of the equator represent the hours of time, and correspond to the degrees of longitude. The figures between the letters express the minutes of time. The edge of the brass meridian is used for drawing a meridian through any place.

10. **Parallels of Latitude** are small circles parallel to the equator, and on the globe are drawn at distances of 10 degrees from each other.

11. The **Latitude** of a place is its distance north or south of the equator, reckoned in degrees on the brass meridian.

12. **Parallels of Celestial Latitude** are small circles drawn on the celestial globe parallel to the ecliptic.

13. **Parallels of Declination** are small circles parallel to the equinoctial on the celestial globe, and are similar to parallels of latitude on a terrestrial globe.

14. The **Tropics** are two small circles parallel to the equator, 23½ degrees from it. The northern is called the Tropic of Cancer, and the southern the Tropic of Capricorn.

15. The **Polar Circles** are two small circles parallel to the equator, and 23½ degrees from the poles. The northern is the Arctic circle, and the southern is the Antarctic.

16. The **Zones.** The surface of the earth is divided by the tropics and polar circles into five parts, called zones. The part lying between the tropics of Cancer and Capricorn is called the Torrid Zone; between the tropic of Cancer and the Arctic circle, the North Temperate Zone; between the tropic of Capricorn and the Antarctic circle, the South Temperate

Zone; between the Arctic circle and the North pole, the North Frigid Zone; between the Antarctic circle and the South pole, the South Frigid Zone.

17. The **Ecliptic** is a great circle representing the sun's apparent path throughout the year. It touches the tropics of Cancer and Capricorn, and is inclined to the equator at an angle of 23½ degrees. The two points where it crosses the equator are called the *Equinoctial Points.*

18. The **Signs of the Zodiac.** The ecliptic is divided into twelve parts of 30 degrees each, called Signs of the Zodiac, each having a particular name and character by which it is designated. There are six northern and six southern ones. The sun appears in the former in our spring and summer months, and in the latter during our autumn and winter months. The days on which the sun enters the different signs are as follows : —

NORTHERN SIGNS OF THE ZODIAC.

Spring Signs.	*Summer Signs.*
Aries, the Ram, March 21.	Cancer, the Crab, June 21.
Taurus, the Bull, April 20.	Leo, the Lion, July 23.
Gemini, the Twins, May 21.	Virgo, the Virgin, August 23.

SOUTHERN SIGNS OF THE ZODIAC.

Autumnal Signs.	*Winter Signs.*
Libra, the Balance, Sept. 23.	Capricornus, the Goat, Dec. 22.
Scorpio, the Scorpion, Oct. 23.	Aquarius, the Waterman, Jan. 20.
Sagittarius, the Archer, Nov. 23.	Pisces, the Fishes, Feb. 19.

19. The **Equinoctial Points** where the equator crosses the ecliptic are Aries and Libra; the former is the Vernal and the latter the Autumnal equinox. When the sun is in either of these points, the days and nights are equal all over the world.

20. The **Solstitial Points** are the points where the ecliptic touches the tropics of Cancer and Capricorn. When the sun

enters Cancer, it is the longest day in the northern and the shortest in the southern hemisphere. On the contrary, when the sun enters Capricorn, it is the shortest day in the northern and the longest in the southern hemisphere.

21. The **Colures** are two great circles passing through the poles. The equinoctial colure passes through the equinoctial points; the other, the solstitial colure, passes through the solstitial points.

22. The **Zenith** is the point in the heavens directly over our heads.

23. The **Nadir** is the point in the heavens directly below our feet.

24. **Antipodes** are the people who live on opposite sides of the earth, and walk feet to feet. Their latitudes, longitudes, days and nights, seasons, are exactly contrary to each other.

25. There are two **Horizons;** the sensible or visible horizon, and the rational or true horizon.

26. The **Sensible Horizon** is that circle in the earth which bounds our view.

27. The **Rational** or **True Horizon** is a great circle of the heavens, everywhere 90 degrees from the zenith.

28. The **Altitude** of an object in the heavens is its distance from the horizon. When the body is on a meridian, such as the sun at noon, its altitude is then called *meridian altitude.*

29. The **Zenith Distance** of a celestial body is its distance from the zenith.

30. The **Quadrant** is a thin, flexible strip of brass, divided upward from 0 to 90 degrees, and downward from 0 to 18 degrees. It can be screwed to the brass meridian. The upper part is used for finding distances between places on the earth, the altitude of heavenly bodies, etc., and the lower for finding the length of twilight.

31. **Almacanters** or **Parallels of Altitude** are imaginary circles

parallel to the horizon, and serve to show the height of the sun, moon, and stars. The circles are not drawn on the globe, but they may be described for any latitude by the quadrant of altitude.

32. **Azimuth** or **Vertical Circles** are great circles passing through the zenith and nadir points, cutting the horizon at right angles. The altitudes of the heavenly bodies are measured on these circles. This is done by screwing the quadrant of altitude on the zenith of the place of observation, and moving the slip of brass until its graduated edge passes through the body.

33. The **Azimuth** of any celestial body is an arc of the horizon lying between a vertical circle passing through the body and the north or south points of the horizon.

34. The **Amplitude** of any celestial body is the distance at which it rises from the east or sets from the west.

35. The **Wooden Horizon,** surrounding the artificial globe, represents the rational horizon. It is usually divided into seven concentric circles: the first is for finding the *amplitude* of heavenly bodies; the second for finding their *azimuth;* the third contains the thirty-two points of the *compass;* the fourth contains the twelve signs of the *zodiac,* with the degrees of each sign; the fifth contains the days of the month, corresponding to every degree of the sun's place in the ecliptic, as indicated in the fourth circle; the sixth contains the equation of time, that is, the difference of time between a clock and a sun-dial; the seventh contains the twelve calendar months.

36. The **Hour Circle** is a flat brass circle turning on the axis of the globe at the pole, and under the brass meridian. It is divided into 24 equal parts representing hours. It is used for finding the difference of time between places, the length of the days, etc. On some globes the hour circle is,

drawn around the pole, and has a brass index which is attached to the axis.

37. The **Declination** of the sun is its distance north or south of the equinoctial. At the equinoxes it has no declination. At the tropic of Cancer it has its greatest northern declination, and at the tropic of Capricorn, its greatest southern declination.

38. The **Right Ascension** of the sun is the distance of the meridian passing through the sun's place in the ecliptic, from the equinoctial point Aries, reckoned in degrees eastward on the equator or equinoctial.

39. The **Analemma** is a diagram resembling the figure 8. It is a scale drawn on the terrestrial globe from one tropic to the other, showing the sun's declination on any day in the year. It contains the months and days and signs of the zodiac, and shows the equation of time, that is, the difference between clock-time and that of the sun-dial.

PROBLEMS ON THE TERRESTRIAL GLOBE.

PROBLEM I. *To find the latitude and longitude of any given place.*

RULE. Bring the given place to the graduated edge of the metallic meridian ; the degree directly over the place is the latitude. The degree on the equator cut by the metallic meridian is the longitude.

EXAMPLES.

What is the latitude and longitude of the following places?

New York.	*Answer:*	Lat.	41° N.	Long.	74° W.
San Francisco.	"	"	37° N.	"	122° W.
Calcutta.	"	"	23° N.	"	89° E.
Rio Janeiro.	"	"	23° S.	"	43° W.
Quito.	"	"	0°	"	79° W

The latitude of the north and of the south pole is 90°. The longitude of the poles is 0°. 90° is the highest latitude that any place can have. 180° is the highest longitude that any place can have. All places on the equator have no latitude. All places on the first meridian have no longitude.

PROBLEM II. *To find any place on the globe having its latitude and longitude given.*

RULE. Find the given longitude on the equator, and bring it to the metallic meridian. Find the given latitude on the metallic meridian, and the place immediately under will be the place required.

EXAMPLES.

What places have about the following latitudes and longitudes?

33° S.	72° W.	*Answer:*	Valparaiso.
9° N.	80° W.	"	Panama.
42° N.	88° W.	"	Chicago.
19° N.	100° W.	"	Mexico.
35° N.	140° E.	"	Yokohama.

PROBLEM III. *To find all those places which have the same latitude as a given place.*

RULE. Bring the given place to the metallic meridian, and find its latitude. Turn the globe slowly round, and all places which pass under the observed latitude will be the ones required.

EXAMPLES.

What places have about the same latitude as Boston?

Answer: Albany, Buffalo, Chicago, Omaha, Constanti- nople, Rome, Marseilles.

All places in the same latitude have the same seasons and the same length of day and night; but, owing to various physical causes (such as the adjoining land and water), they may not have the same climate.

PROBLEM IV. *To find all those places which have the same longitude as a given place.*

RULE. Bring the place to the metallic meridian. All places under the edge of the metallic meridian, from pole to pole, have the same longitude.

People living in the same longitude have noon and all of the hours of the day alike; their clocks all agree; but they all have sunrise and sunset at different hours from one another, depending on their latitude.

EXAMPLES.

What places have about the same longitude as Copenhagen?

Answer: Berlin, Venice, Rome, Palermo, Tripoli, mouth of the Congo River.

What people have nearly the same time as the people of Massachusetts?

Answer: Those in Quebec, Hayti, Venezuela, Colombia, Ecuador, Peru, and Chili.

PROBLEM V. *To find the distance between two places.*

RULE. Lay the edge of the quadrant of altitude over the two places, so that the point marked 0 may be over one of them; the number of degrees over the other place will be the number of degrees they are apart. Multiply the number of degrees by 60 for the geographical miles, or by 69½ for the English or statute miles. Or take the distance between the two places with a thread; apply that distance to the equator; this will show the number of degrees in the distance; then multiply as before for the miles.

EXAMPLES.

What is the distance between

		Degrees.	Geog. Miles.	Eng. Miles.
Portland and San Francisco?	*Answer:*	39½	2370	2732
London " Constantinople?	"	22	1320	1522
Liverpool " Cairo?	"	34	2040	2352

PROBLEM VI. *The hour of the day being given at one place, to find what hour it is at any other place.*

RULE. Bring the place at which the time is given to the metallic meridian; turn the hour circle until the given hour comes to the metallic meridian, or set the hour index to the given hour; turn the globe until the other place comes under the metallic meridian, and the hour on the hour circle, which is under the metallic meridian or under the index, will be the time required.

Or thus by calculation.

RULE. Find the difference in longitude between the two places, allow an hour for every 15 degrees and 4 minutes for every degree, and the time thus obtained will be the difference of time between the two places. If the place at which the time is required lies to the east of the given place, this difference of time must be added to find the time at the place required; but if it lies to the west, it must be subtracted.

EXAMPLES.

When it is 3 o'clock in the afternoon at London, what time is it at St. Petersburgh?

Answer: 5 o'clock in the afternoon.

Or by calculation. The difference in longitude is 30°; divided by 15 gives just 2 hours difference of time. St. Petersburgh being east of London, this 2 hours must be added to the London time, which gives us 5 o'clock in the afternoon.

When it is 2 o'clock in the afternoon at Cairo, what time is it at New York?

Answer: 7 o'clock in the morning.

By calculation. Longitude, Cairo,   31° E.
                   "   New York, 74° W.

Difference of longitude, 105°, divided by 15 gives 7, the difference in hours.

New York being west of Cairo, these 7 hours must be subtracted from Cairo time, and 7 from 2 o'clock in the afternoon is 7 o'clock in the morning.

PROBLEM VII.   *The time of any two places, and one of the places being given, to find the longitude of the other place.*

RULE.   Bring the given place to the metallic meridian, set the hour index at the given hour of the place, turn the globe until the other given hour comes under the metallic meridian, and the degree on the equator cut by the metallic meridian will be the longitude.

Or by calculation.

RULE.   Allow 15° difference of longitude for every hour of time, or 1° for every 4 minutes of time.

EXAMPLES.

When it is 4 o'clock in the afternoon at a certain place, it is noon at London; required the longitude of the place.

Answer: 60° east longitude.

By calculation. 4 hours of time, at 15° for each hour, gives 60°, the difference of longitude. As the hour at London is earlier than at the other place, it follows that the place must be 60° to the east of London; or, as London has 0° for longitude, the place must have 60° east longitude.

When it is noon at Boston, at what places is it 10 o'clock in the morning.

Answer: All places in longitude 100° west, as the middle of Nebraska, Kansas, Texas, and the city of Mexico.

PROBLEM VIII. *To find the length of a degree in any given parallel of latitude.*

RULE. Lay the edge of the quadrant of altitude along the given parallel; take the number of degrees upon it intercepted between any two meridians (15° apart), and that number multiplied by 4 will give the number of geographical miles contained in a degree of the given parallel. To find the number of English miles, multiply the number of degrees by 69⅓, and divide by 15, or, what is the same thing, multiply the number of degrees by 4.6.

EXAMPLES.

How many geographical and English miles are there in a degree on the 50th parallel of latitude?

Answer: The distance between two meridians 15° apart on the 50th parallel is 9¾° of the equator.

$$9\frac{3}{4} \times 4 \quad = 39 \quad \text{geographical miles.}$$
$$9\frac{3}{4} \times 4.6 = 44.85 \text{ statute miles.}$$

What is the length of a degree on the parallel of 30°?

Answer: 15° parallel of 30° = 13° on the equator.

$$13 \times 4 \quad = 52 \quad \text{geographical miles.}$$
$$13 \times 4.6 = 59.8 \text{ statute miles.}$$

PROBLEM IX. *To find the Antipodes of a given place.*

RULE. Bring the given place to the metallic meridian; set the index of the hour circle at 12, or bring 12 on the hour circle to the metallic meridian; turn the globe half round, or until the index points to the other 12; then, under the same degree of latitude with the given place, but in the opposite hemisphere, will be the place of the Antipodes.

EXAMPLES.

Required the Antipodes of the following places: —

London.	*Answer:*	Antipodes Island, near New Zealand.
Spain.	"	New Zealand.
Chili.	"	China.
Bermudas Islands.	"	South-west part of West Australia.

PROBLEM X.   *To rectify the globe for any given place.*

RULE.   Elevate or raise the north or south pole as many degrees above the wooden horizon as are equal to the latitude of the place, and bring the given place to the metallic meridian.   If the given place is in north latitude, the north pole must be elevated; if in south latitude, the south pole.   In elevating either pole, the degrees must be counted from the pole to be elevated toward the equator.

EXAMPLES

Rectify the globe for Boston.

Boston is in latitude 42½° north; therefore elevate the north pole 42½° above the wooden horizon, and turn the globe until Boston comes to the edge of the metallic meridian.

Rectify the globe for Rio Janeiro.

Rio Janeiro is 23½° south latitude.   Elevate the south pole 23½° above the wooden horizon, and turn the globe until Rio Janeiro comes to the edge of the metallic meridian.

NOTE.   When the globe is rectified for any place, the place is in the zenith of the globe; that is, it is everywhere 90° from the wooden horizon, and the wooden horizon becomes the true horizon of the place.

Now, if the stand of the globe is made to occupy a horizontal position, and the north and south points of the wooden horizon are made to correspond with the north and south points of the compass, the globe is said to be set. In this position the axis of the globe is parallel with the axis of the earth, the equator of the globe to the equator of the earth, the parallels of the globe to the parallels of the earth; and the globe may be turned, so that the ecliptic on the globe shall be parallel to the ecliptic in the heavens on any day in the year.

PROBLEM XI. *To find the sun's place in the ecliptic for any given day.*

RULE. Find the month, and the mark corresponding to the day of that month, in the outer circle of the wooden horizon; then the coincident mark in the circle containing the signs of the zodiac will give the sun's place in the ecliptic, which may then be found upon the globe.

In JOSLIN'S GLOBES the ecliptic is divided also into the months and the days of the month, so that any required day may be found directly on the ecliptic.

PROBLEM XII. *To find the sun's declination for any given day, and also to find the places to which the sun will be vertical on that day.*

RULE. Find the sun's place in the ecliptic for the given day; bring that point in the ecliptic to the metallic meridian, and the degree directly over it on the metallic meridian is the declination, north or south. Turn the globe around, and every place which passes under that degree of the metallic meridian will have the sun vertical on that day.

The declination of the sun gives the latitude of the places which will have the sun vertical on that day. The sun can be vertical only to places within the torrid zone.

Or the declination may be found by bringing the given day on the analemma to the metallic meridian, and the degree on the meridian over the day on the analemma will be the declination.

EXAMPLES.

What is the declination of the sun on the 21st of June, and what is the latitude of the places that will have the sun vertical on that day?

Answer: 23½° North Declination.
23½° North Latitude.

What is the sun's declination on the following days?

Sept. 12. *Answer:* 4½° North Declination.
Dec. 10.   "   22½° South   "
Jan. 1.   "   23° South   "
April 15.   "   10° North   "

PROBLEM XIII. *To find the hour at which the sun rises and sets at a given place, for any given day. Also, to find the amplitude of the sun for that day.*

RULE. Rectify the globe for the latitude of the place by Problem X. Find the sun's place in the ecliptic, and bring it to the metallic meridian. Set the index of the hour circle at 12. Turn the globe until the sun's place comes to the eastern edge of the wooden horizon, and the index will then show the hour at which the sun rises; then turn the globe until the sun's place comes to the western edge of the wooden horizon, when the index will show the hour at which the sun sets.

REMARK. 1. The length of the day is found by doubling the hour of sunset.

2. The length of the night is found by doubling the hour of sunrise.

3. To find the amplitude of the sun, observe the degree of amplitude on the wooden horizon, which is cut by the sun's place in the ecliptic at the time of rising or setting.

EXAMPLES.

At what time will the sun rise and set at London on the 21st of December? What is the length of the day and night at that time, and what is the amplitude of the sun?

Answer: The sun rises at ¼ past 8.
   The sun sets at ¼ before 4.
   Length of day, 7½ hours.
   Length of night, 16½ hours.
   Sun's amplitude, 39° south of east.

What is the length of the longest day at St. Petersburgh?
How far from the east point of the horizon does the sun rise
on that day?

Answer: Length of day, 18¼ hours.
   Sun's amplitude, 52° north of east.

What is the length of the shortest day in New York?

Answer: Length of day, 9 hours.

Show that the day is always 12 hours long at the equator.

Show that the 21st of June is the longest day to the people
of the northern hemisphere, and that the 21st of December
is their shortest.

PROBLEM XIV. *To find the sun's meridian altitude at a
given place on a given day.*

RULE. Rectify the globe for the latitude of the place; bring the
sun's place in the ecliptic for the given day to the metallic meridian;
count the number of degrees on the metallic meridian, between the sun's
place and the wooden horizon, for the meridian altitude required.

Or thus: Find the declination of the sun for the day, and add to it
the co-latitude of the place when the declination and the co-latitude are
of the same name, but subtract it when they are of different names.

EXAMPLES.

What is the sun's meridian altitude at Boston on the 21st
of June?

Answer: 71°. This is the greatest elevation of the sun
   above the horizon at Boston.

By calculation. The latitude and declination are both north. The declination of the sun on this day is $23\frac{1}{2}°$ north, and the co-latitude is $90° - 42\frac{1}{2}° = 47\frac{1}{2}°$; therefore the meridian altitude is $23\frac{1}{2}° + 47\frac{1}{2}° = 71°$.

What is the sun's meridian altitude at Boston on December 21?

Answer: 24°. This is the least meridian altitude of the sun to the people of Boston.

By calculation. Here the declination is south and the latitude north, therefore we have the meridian altitude $47\frac{1}{2}° - 23\frac{1}{2}° = 24°$.

What would be the meridian altitude of the sun on the 21st of June at the following places?

North Pole. *Answer:* $23\frac{1}{2}°$.
Arctic Circle. " 47°.
Equator. " $66\frac{1}{2}°$, or $23\frac{1}{2}°$ from the zenith.

PROBLEM XV. *To find the sun's altitude and azimuth at any given place on any given day and hour.*

RULE. Rectify the globe for the latitude of the place; bring the sun's place in the ecliptic to the metallic meridian; set the index at 12; turn the globe until the index points to the given hour; fix the quadrant of altitude on the metallic meridian, at the degree of latitude of the given place, and lay its graduated edge over the sun's place; then count the number of degrees on the quadrant between this point and the wooden horizon, and it will give the altitude required. The number of degrees on the wooden horizon, counting from the north or south point of it, to the point where the graduated edge of the quadrant cuts it, will be the azimuth.

EXAMPLES.

What is the sun's altitude and azimuth at London on the 5th of May at 7 o'clock in the morning?

Answer: Altitude, $21\frac{1}{2}°$.
Azimuth, 90° from the north.

What is the sun's altitude and azimuth at St. Petersburgh on July 2 at 4 P.M.

Answer: Altitude, 35°.

Azimuth, 75° from the south.

PROBLEM XVI. *The hour and day at any particular place being given, to find the place where the sun is then vertical.*

RULE. Find the sun's declination of the given day (Problem XII.); bring the given place to the metallic meridian ; set the index to the given hour; turn the globe until the index points to 12 noon. The place under the metallic meridian whose latitude is the same as the sun's declination will have the sun vertical at the hour given. This also shows that all places under the metallic meridian will have noon at the same time.

EXAMPLES.

To what place will the sun be vertical on the 7th of January when it is ¾ to 3 in the afternoon at London?

Answer: Rio Janeiro.

To what place will the sun be vertical when it is 2 o'clock in the afternoon of May 15 at Boston?

Answer: City of Mexico.

PROBLEM XVII. *To find the two days in the year in which the sun will be vertical to any given place in the torrid zone.*

RULE. Bring the given place to the metallic meridian, and observe its latitude. Bring the analemma to the metallic meridian, and the two days on it that come under that latitude are the days required.

EXAMPLES.

On what two days of the year will the sun be vertical at Aspinwall?

Answer: April 2 and August 30.

On what two days will the sun be vertical at Calcutta?

Answer: June 10 and July 4.

PROBLEM XVIII. *The hour and day at a particular place being given, to find the places where the sun is then rising or setting; and also places where it is noon or midnight.*

RULE. Find the sun's declination for the given day; elevate the north or south pole (according as the sun's declination is north or south) as many degrees above the wooden horizon as are equal to the sun's declination; bring the given place to the metallic meridian, and set the index to the given hour; turn the globe until the index points to 12 noon. Then to all places above the wooden horizon it will be day, and to all places beneath it it will be night; all places on the western edge of the wooden horizon will have the sun rising, and all places on the eastern edge will have it setting; all places under the upper half of the metallic meridian will have noon, and all those under the lower half will have midnight. All places not more than 18° below the western edge of the horizon will have morning twilight, and all places not more than 18° below its eastern edge will have evening twilight.

EXAMPLES.

When it is 8 o'clock in the morning at Boston on the 23d of June, where is the sun rising and setting? and where is it noon and where midnight?

> *Answer:* The sun is rising at San Francisco and the Pacific coast States, the southern part of Chili, and at Patagonia; it is setting at Calcutta, the middle of the Chinese Empire, and the eastern part of Siberia. It is nearly noon at Ireland, Portugal, and the extreme western part of Africa; it is midnight at the Loyalty Islands and New Zealand.

When it is 4 o'clock in the afternoon at London on the 25th of April, where is the sun rising, setting, etc.?

> *Answer:* Rising at Sandwich Islands.
> Setting at Cape of Good Hope.
> Noon at Nova Scotia, Venezuela, and Buenos Ayres.
> Midnight at Australia and China.

PROBLEM XIX. *Any place in the north frigid zone being given, to find how long the sun shines there without setting, and how long he is invisible.*

RULE. Rectify the globe for the latitude of the place; bring the ascending signs of the ecliptic to the north point of the horizon, and see what day of the ecliptic is cut by that point; then from that day the sun begins to shine without setting. Now bring the descending signs of the ecliptic to the north point of the horizon, and see what day of the ecliptic is cut by that point; then on that day the sun ceases to shine without setting. By proceeding in the same way with the southern point of the horizon, we may find the beginning and end of the time during which the sun is invisible.

EXAMPLES.

How long does the sun shine without setting at Uppernavik in Greenland, latitude 72½° north, and how long is he invisible?

> *Answer:* It begins to shine continually on the 9th of May, and ceases to shine continually on the 4th of August.
>
> The longest day is therefore 87 days long; that is, the sun shines without setting for 87 days.
>
> The time during which the sun will be invisible extends from the 10th of November to February 1.
>
> The longest night is therefore 83 days long; that is, the sun is never seen during this 83 days.

PROBLEM XX. *To find the beginning, end, and duration of twilight at any given place on any given day.*

RULE. Rectify the globe for the latitude of the place (Problem X.); screw the quadrant of altitude upon the metallic meridian over the given latitude; bring the sun's place in the ecliptic on the given day to the metallic meridian; set the hour circle at 12; turn the globe westward until the sun's place comes to the western edge of the wooden horizon;

then the hour circle will show the time of the sun's setting and the beginning of evening twilight. Continue turning the globe until the sun's place is 18° below the horizon, measured on the quadrant of altitude; then the hour circle will show the time at which the evening twilight ends. The duration of twilight is equal to the difference between the time at which it begins and the time at which it ends.

The time at which evening twilight ends, subtracted from 12, will give the time of the beginning of morning twilight, which is of the same length as evening twilight.

EXAMPLES.

Required the beginning, end, and duration of evening and morning twilight at London on the 23d of September.

> *Answer:* Evening twilight begins at 6 o'clock and ends at 8 o'clock; duration, 2 hours. Morning twilight begins at 4 o'clock and ends at 6 o'clock.

> *Solution:*

Evening twilight ends	8 h.
" " begins	6 h.
Duration of twilight	2 h.
	12 h.
Evening twilight ends	8 h.
Morning twilight begins	4 h.
Duration of twilight	2 h.
Morning twilight ends	6 h.

Required the duration of twilight at Boston on June 1.

Answer: 2¾ hours.

PROBLEM XXI. *The sun's meridian altitude and the day of the month being given, to find the latitude of the place.*

RULE. Bring the sun's place in the ecliptic to the metallic meridian; then, if the sun was south of the observer when the altitude was taken, elevate the sun's place as many degrees above the south point of the wooden horizon as are equal to the sun's meridian altitude; the elevation of the north pole above the horizon will give the latitude of the place. If the sun was north of the observer when the altitude was taken, elevate the sun's place as many degrees above the north point of the horizon as are equal to the sun's meridian altitude; the elevation of the south pole will give the latitude of the place.

EXAMPLES.

On the 21st of June the meridian altitude of the sun was observed to be 69½°, and south of the observer; what was the latitude of the place?

Answer : 44° north.

December 21 the meridian altitude of the sun was 25°, and south of the observer; what was the latitude of the place?

Answer : 41½° north.

May 10 the sun's meridian altitude was observed to be 30° north of the observer; what was the latitude of the place?

Answer : 42¼° south.

PROBLEM XXII. *To find all places at which a solar or lunar eclipse is visible at the same instant, the day and hour being given when it is visible at a certain place.*

RULE. Find the place to which the sun is vertical at the given time; bring the place to the metallic meridian, and rectify the globe to the latitude of that place; then at all places within 70° of this place an eclipse of the sun *may* be visible, especially if it be a total eclipse. If it be a lunar eclipse, it will be visible to all those places below the wooden horizon.

EXAMPLES.

There was an eclipse of the sun October 9, 1847, at 7½ o'clock in the morning, at London; at what places might it be visible?

Answer: London, Hindoostan, Arabia, Egypt, etc.

There was an eclipse of the moon January 26, 1842, at 6 o'clock in the afternoon, at London; at what places was it visible?

Answer: Europe, Africa, part of Asia, and South America.

There was an eclipse of the moon January 7, 1852, at 6½ o'clock in the morning, at London; at what places was it visible?

Answer: England, France, Spain, North and South America.

PROBLEM XXIII. *To place the terrestrial globe in the sunshine at any given place, so that it will represent the actual position of the earth at that time with respect to the sun.*

RULE. Place the globe so that the wooden horizon shall be in a horizontal position, and its north and south points in a line exactly north and south, the north to the north; bring the given place to the metallic meridian, and rectify the globe to its latitude. All the lines on the globe are then in the position described under Problem X.

PROBLEM XXIV. *To construct a horizontal sun-dial by the globe for any given latitude.*

RULE. Set the globe as in Problem XXII., and bring the first point of Aries (the meridian of Greenwich) to the metallic meridian. Prepare a smooth board about 6 inches wider than the diameter of the globe. On this board describe a circle whose diameter is exactly the same as the diameter of the globe. At the extremities of a diameter of this circle mark a north and south point. Regard these two points as cut by the plane of the first meridian. Mark the north point 12, which will indicate the hour of noon. With a pair of dividers take the exact distances between each two meridians, 15° apart, at the points where they are cut by the horizon, beginning at the north point of the horizon and going each way. Transfer these distances to the circumference of the circle on the board, making a point to correspond with each meridian. Number the points from 12 toward the west 11–10–9 for the morning hours, and toward the east 1–2–3–4–5 for the evening hours. No more points may be made than equal the number of hours in the longest day at the given place. From the centre of the circle draw a radius to each point in the circumference. In the centre fix a pin inclined toward the north point, or 12, as many degrees as are equal to the latitude of the place, and of such length that its shortest shadow will reach the circumference. This board placed exactly horizontal in the sunshine, with its north and south points in a line exactly north and south, will constitute a horizontal sun-dial.

PROBLEM XXV. *To illustrate the three positions of the sphere, RIGHT, PARALLEL, and OBLIQUE, so as to show the aspect of the sun, etc., at different times of the year.*

The **Right Sphere.** The people at the equator have this sphere; the north polar star always appears in their horizon. To place the globe in this position bring the two poles to the wooden horizon; turn the globe round; then the following facts may be readily shown. At the equator the days are always 12 hours long, whatever may be the position of the sun in the ecliptic; for the sun and all the heavenly bodies will appear to revolve round the earth in circles parallel to the equinoctial, and the diurnal arc above the horizon will always be equal to that which is below it. The whole of the heavens may be seen at the equator in the course of the day, and in a year all the stars in the heavens may be seen.

The **Parallel Sphere.** The people at the poles, if there were any, would have this sphere; at the north pole, the north polar star would appear exactly overhead. To place the globe in this position, elevate the north pole 90° above the horizon, or, what is the same thing, make the equator to coincide with the wooden horizon. At the poles, during six months of the year, the sun shines without setting, and during the other six months he never appears above the horizon. At the poles the heavenly bodies appear to move in circles parallel to the horizon; they appear to move entirely around it every 24 hours. The sun appears to move in the form of a spiral, higher each day, for three months, till he reaches his greatest declination; and then, in a similar manner, lower and lower, for three months, till he goes below the horizon. But there will be twilight until the sun is 18° below the horizon. At the poles an observer can see only those stars that are in his hemisphere. Near the poles the stars do not set, but appear to revolve around the pole, going down each day toward the horizon, but never below it.

The **Oblique Sphere.** All people on the earth, excepting those at the equator and the poles, have this position of the sphere. In this case the horizon cuts the equator obliquely. To place the globe in this position, elevate the pole to the latitude of the place of the observer. Take Boston, for example, and elevate the north pole to the latitude of Boston. To the people of Boston, for six months of the year, the days are more than 12 hours long, and for the other six months they are less than 12 hours long. On the 21st of March the sun shines perpendicularly over the equator, and the days and nights are equal in length all over the globe; as the sun's northern declination increases the days increase in length, for the diurnal arcs described by the sun are unequally divided by the horizon. When the sun has attained its greatest northern declination, June 21, the days have attained their greatest length, but they will be the shortest to the people of the southern hemisphere. After this, the sun's northern declination gradually decreases, and the days also decrease in length. When the sun arrives at the autumnal equinox, September 22, the days and nights are again of equal length. After this, the days become shorter and shorter as the sun's southern declination increases, until it has attained its greatest southern declination, December 21. Then the days will be shortest with us, but longest to the people of the southern hemisphere. After this, our days increase in length, and, when the sun again arrives at the vernal equinox, the days and nights are again equal.

The duration of twilight is greater with us than at the equator, because with us the diurnal arc of the sun cuts the horizon obliquely, which causes it to take a longer time to get 18° below the horizon ; whereas, at the equator, the sun sinks perpendicularly below the horizon, which shortens the duration of twilight.

The people that live in the northern hemisphere can never see those stars which lie toward the south polar star, and the people in the southern hemisphere can never see those stars which lie toward the north polar star ; but, as already noted, a person at the equator may see all the stars in the heavens in the course of the year.

THE CELESTIAL GLOBE.

1. The **Celestial Globe** is constructed to represent the aspect of the heavens; all the stars are laid down on its surface according to their relative situations; and the various imaginary circles and points upon the terrestrial globe are supposed to be transferred to the celestial one. The rotary motion of this globe, from east to west, represents the apparent diurnal motion of the sun and stars to a spectator supposed to be situated in the centre of the globe.

2. The **Latitude and Longitude of a Star or Planet.** The latitude of a body on the celestial globe is its distance from the ecliptic, north or south, measured in degrees on a great circle passing through the body and the pole of the ecliptic; and the longitude is the distance of the point, where the great circle cuts the ecliptic, from the first point of Aries. Latitude and longitude are referred to the ecliptic on the celestial globe, but on the terrestrial globe they are referred to the equator.

3. The **Declination and Right Ascension** of a heavenly body. The declination of a body is its distance from the equinoctial, north or south, measured in degrees on a meridian passing through the body; and the right ascension is the distance of the point where this meridian cuts the equinoctial, from the first point of Aries. The right ascension of a body is sometimes expressed in hours, making the usual allowance of one hour of time for 15° of distance.

PROBLEMS ON THE CELESTIAL GLOBE.

PROBLEM I. *To find the right ascension and declination of the sun or of a star.*

RULE. Bring the sun's place in the ecliptic, or the given star, to the metallic meridian; the degree over it is the declination, and the degree on the equator cut by the metallic meridian gives the right ascension.

EXAMPLES.

1. Required the right ascension and declination of Regulus, in the constellation of the Lion.

Answer: Right ascension, 150°; Declination, 12° 47' north.

Required the right ascension and declination of the following stars: —

2. Capella, in the constellation of Auriga.
3. Dubhe,   "   "   "   the Great Bear.
4. Aldebaran, "   "   "   Taurus.
5. Arcturus, "   "   "   Bootes.

Answers:

2. Right Ascension, 76°.   Declination, 45° 49' north.
3.   "   "   163° 15'.   "   62° 36'   "
4.   "   "   66°.   "   16° 10'   "
5.   "   "   212°.   "   20° 3'   "

PROBLEM II. *The right ascension and declination of a heavenly body being given, to find its place on the globe.*

RULE. Bring the given degree (or given time) of right ascension to the metallic meridian; then under the given degree of declination reckoned on the metallic meridian you will find the place of the body.

EXAMPLES.

1. Required the star whose right ascension is 76° 45', or 5 hours 7 minutes, and declination 8° 24' south.

Answer: Rigal, a star of the first magnitude in the constellation of Orion.

What stars have the following positions?

	Right Ascension.	Declination.
2.	261° 30' or 17 h. 26 min.	52° 25' north.
3.	6 h. 38 min.	16° 29' south.
4.	19 h. 43 min.	8° 26' north.
5.	7 h. 35 min.	28° 26' north.

Answers :

2. Alwaid, in the constellation of Draco.
3. Sirius,   "   "   "   the Great Dog.
4. Al Tair,   "   "   "   the Eagle.
5. Pollux,   "   "   "   the South Twin.

PROBLEM III.   *To find the latitude and longitude of any star.*

RULE.   Bring the pole of the ecliptic to the metallic meridian; fix the quadrant of altitude over the pole, and move the quadrant till its edge comes over the star; then the degree of the quadrant over the star is the latitude, and the number of degrees between the edge of the quadrant and the first point of Aries, reckoned on the ecliptic, is the longitude.

EXAMPLES.

What is the latitude and longitude of Aldebaran, in the constellation of Taurus.

Answer : Latitude, 5° 28' south.   Longitude, 2 signs, 6° 53'.

What is the latitude and longitude of Pollux in Gemini?

Answer : Latitude, 6° 30' north.   Longitude, 3 signs, 21°.

PROBLEM IV.   *The day and hour and the latitude of the place being given, to place the celestial globe so as to represent the appearance of the heavens at that place and time.*

RULE.   Rectify the globe to the latitude of the place; bring the sun's place in the ecliptic to the metallic meridian; set the hour circle to 12 (recollect this is 12 noon); turn the globe till the hour circle points to the given hour of the day; then in this position the stars figured on the globe will exactly correspond with the actual appearance of the stars in the heavens.

PROBLEM V. *The day and hour and the latitude of the place being given, to find what stars are rising, setting, and culminating.*

RULE. Rectify the globe for the latitude of the place; bring the sun's place in the ecliptic to the metallic meridian; put the hour circle to 12 noon; turn the globe till the hour circle indicates the given hour of the day: then all the stars on the eastern semicircle will be rising; those on the western semicircle will be setting; those under the metallic meridian will be culminating, or in their southing; and the stars above the wooden horizon will be visible at the given time and place.

To determine those stars which never set. Turn the globe on its axis; then those stars which do not go below the wooden horizon never set at the given place.

EXAMPLES.

To find the constellations which are rising, setting, and culminating, on January 20, at 2 o'clock in the morning, at London.

> *Answer :* The constellations of Lyra, etc., are rising; Andromeda, etc., are setting; and the Great Bear, etc., are on the meridian.

To find the stars which are rising, setting, and culminating, on the 8th of February, at 9 o'clock in the evening, at London.

> *Answer :* Alpheta, in the Northern Crown, is rising; Arcturus, in Bootes, is a little above the horizon; Sirius is on the meridian; Markab, in Pegasus, is just below the western horizon.

PROBLEM VI. *To find the time when any star will rise, come to the meridian, and set, on any given day, at any given place.*

RULE. Rectify the globe to the latitude of the place; bring the sun's place in the ecliptic to the metallic meridian; set the hour circle to 12 noon; turn the globe till the given star comes to the eastern edge of the wooden horizon; then the hour circle will show the time of rising: turn the globe till the star comes to the metallic meridian, and the hour circle will show the time of its culminating, or southing; turn the globe till the star comes to the western edge of the wooden horizon, and the hour circle will show the time of setting.

EXAMPLES.

At what time will Arcturus, in the constellation of Bootes, rise, culminate, and set, at London, on the 7th of September?

> *Answer:* Arcturus will rise at 7 o'clock in the morning, culminate at 3 o'clock in the afternoon, and set at 11 o'clock at night.

At what time will Aldebaran, in the constellation of Taurus, rise, culminate, and set, at Edinburgh, on Nov. 26?

> *Answer:* Aldebaran will rise at 4½ o'clock in the afternoon, culminate at 12¼ o'clock at night, and set at 8 o'clock the next morning.

PROBLEM VII. *The day of the month, the latitude of the place, and the altitude of a star being given, to find the hour of the night.*

RULE. Rectify the globe to the latitude of the place; bring the sun's place in the ecliptic to the metallic meridian; set the hour circle to 12 noon; screw the quadrant of altitude to the zenith, and turn it to that side of the meridian on which the star was observed; move the globe and the quadrant till the star is on the degree of the quadrant equal to the given altitude, then the hour circle will show the hour required.

At Rome, on December 2, the star Capella, in the constellation of Auriga, was observed to be 42° above the horizon; required the hour.

Answer : 5 o'clock in the morning.

At London, on December 29, the star Deneb, in the tail of the Lion, was found to be 40° above the horizon and east of the meridian; required the hour.

Answer : About 2.15 o'clock in the morning.

PROBLEM VIII. *Given the year and the day, to find the place of a planet on the globe.*

RULE. Bring the sun's place in the ecliptic to the metallic meridian; set the hour circle to 12 noon; find in the Nautical Almanac the time when the planet passes the meridian on the given day, and turn the globe till the index of the hour circle points to the hour thus found; find in the Almanac the declination of the planet for the same day; then, under this declination, found on the metallic meridian, is the place of the planet.

Style 3.

Joslin's Bronze Pedestal Stand.

JOSLIN'S BRONZE PEDESTAL STAND.

Style 3.

Mounted in this manner, the globe is brought to a convenient height for use while sitting, and, at the same time, presents an ornamental appearance, adapting it to the parlor and library as well as to the school-room. It is furnished with horizon, graduated full brass nickel-plated meridian, hour dial, etc.

The stand is of bronzed iron, and of such design as to combine great strength with light weight and symmetrical appearance. Being mounted upon brass castors, can be readily moved to any position.

PRICES.

18-inch Globe, 43 inches high   .   .   . $80.00
16 "   "   42½ "   "   .   . 62.50
12 "   "   38½ "   "   .   .   . 37.50

Globe with Celestial Map, same price.

Style 6.

Joslin's Tripod Stand.

JOSLIN'S TRIPOD STAND.

Style 6.

This style of mounting was gotten up particularly for parlor and library use, many persons objecting to an iron stand. It makes a very light, strong, and ornamental stand, and will look well with any furniture. The arms that support the ball and horizon are japanned and decorated, and pivoted the same as in all rotary globes. The legs are japanned with a little decorating, and screw into the socket supporting the arms by a polished brass cap-piece fastened to their top.

PRICES.

18-inch Globe	$78.00
16 " "	60.00
12 " "	37.50

Globe with Celestial Map, same price.

JOSLIN'S LOW BRONZE STAND.

Style 4.

This style, with black walnut horizon, graduated full brass meridian, hour dial, etc., is mounted upon a light bronzed stand of neat and appropriate design.

The arms which support the horizon are pivoted to the base, thus allowing any portion of the globe to be turned to the student without changing the position of the base itself, a very desirable arrangement.

PRICES.

16-inch Globe	$50.00
12 " "	25.00
10 " "	18.00

Globe with Celestial Map, same price.

JOSLIN'S FULL WOOD STAND.

Style 5.

Mounted upon a substantially made cherry wood stand, with horizon, graduated full brass meridian, hour dial, and index, this globe has all the appliances for use in the solution of problems. It is well adapted to all grades of schools.

PRICES.

16-inch Globe	. . . . . .	$45.00
12 " "	. . . . . .	22.00
10 " "	. . . . . .	17.00
6 " "	. . . . . .	10.00

Globe with Celestial Map, same price.

JOSLIN'S LOW TRIPOD STAND.

Style 8.

Mounted upon three light, neat, bronzed iron legs (preventing any shrinking and coming apart, as sometimes happens in wooden stands), with black walnut horizon, graduated full brass meridian, hour dial, and index. Everything is as accurate as in the highest priced globe ever made.

PRICES.

12-inch Globe $22.00
10   "   " 17.00

Globe with Celestial Map, same price.

JOSLIN'S SEMI-CIRCLE STAND.

Style 1.

Polished black walnut stand, with graduated brass semi-meridian. For those who use the globe for reference only, and who never desire to work problems, this style is neat and most appropriate.

PRICES.

12-inch Globe	.	.	.	.	.	. $17.00
10 " "	.	.	.	.	.	. 12.00
6 " "	.	.	.	.	.	. 5.00

Globe with Celestial Map, same price.

JOSLIN'S TELLURIC GLOBE.

This style was specially designed to furnish a *simple* means of illustrating the causes of the Changes of the Seasons and of the numerous other phenomena which are related to them. Their success in accomplishing this much desired end is fully attested by the high commendations of teachers from all sections of the country.

Each globe is accompanied with a printed manual of 30 pages, giving a complete description of the globe and its various uses, with illustrative problems.

PRICE.

6-inch Globe $15.00

.